# Santa School
## Because He Can't Be Everywhere

*Jennifer Andrews*

Santa School
Copyright © 2020 by Jennifer Andrews

All rights reserved. No part of this publication may be reproduced, distributed, or transmitted in any form or by any means, including photocopying, recording, or other electronic or mechanical methods, without the prior written permission of the author, except in the case of brief quotations embodied in critical reviews and certain other non-commercial uses permitted by copyright law.

Tellwell Talent
www.tellwell.ca

ISBN
978-0-2288-1088-9 (Hardcover)
978-0-2288-1089-6 (Paperback)

This book is dedicated to my dad who had to go way too soon, and who taught me what finding the real Santa means.

Without him I would not have experienced magic or dreams or how to find them.

This is also dedicated to my family, my people, my clan. Without them, I would be lost. Also, a special tribute to my 'day ones': my brothers and sister, my sisters in law and my brother in law, my nephews and nieces, my husband, and my children who love me and believe in me and who also understand what magic is and how important it is to have it together, no matter what.

Of course, this is also dedicated to you, Santa. XO

I am Jennifer, Santa's personally appointed chief elf. I happen to know a lot about Santa and I have written this true story, which is also a Santa detection manual, written just for you. Kids spend the most time visiting with Santa so I figured it was a good idea that you learned all of the Santa secrets there are to know. I hope you teach your friends what you learn here.

I am going to let you in on giant Santa secrets. We all talk about the Santa at the mall and we hear people ask each other if they think he's the "real" one or not. The same thing happens during parades and all kinds of parties. People are always trying to figure out if the real Santa, if the guy they're waiting to have their picture taken with, is the real deal. You've probably wondered, what does the REAL SANTA really mean anyway? Why are there so many of him? How will I actually know if I've found the legit*, REAL SANTA?

When I was little, my dad taught me what REAL SANTA means. Now, I want to tell you about an acronym* that defines REAL SANTA.

legit - actual and authentic

acronym - an abbreviation formed from the first letters of other words and pronounced as a word

The REAL SANTA is:

**R**emarkable

**E**xceptional

**A**uthentic

**L**istener

**S**ervice

**A**ccepting

**N**oble

**T**rustworthy

**A**geless

I am a very lucky girl. My dad was Santa's cousin. That makes me Santa's first cousin once removed. So, it turns out that I am Santa's cousin too!

When I was a little girl, my brothers and sister and I would sit on Santa's knee. Well, we thought it was Santa, but it was actually our very own dad! What we did not know at the time, was that our dad was one of Santa's regional representatives. What this means is that the REAL SANTA trained our dad to be so much like him that we couldn't even tell the difference between our dad who was dressed like Santa and Santa himself.

Our dad even helped Santa by keeping an extra suit for him right at our house. We had a very special closet that was just for Santa and his beautiful soft suit hung there all year. Occasionally, we kids would go and check on it, just to see it. We would pet the red velvet and feel the soft fur. Our dad said that every year on Christmas Eve, Santa would need a little break from all of his travels. He would come to our house, take that break and change into a fresh suit. This made total sense because going in and out of chimneys all over the world had to mess up your clothes in a big way!

December
21ST

Santa cannot be everywhere all of the time. He is just one little elf. Well, he is actually the big jolly captain of all of the elves but still, he cannot be everywhere in one moment. He is powerful, and he can do a lot, but he alone cannot do everything.

So, he makes sure that his cousins, his brothers in red, his "regional representatives," become his best trained, most well-equipped, authentic helpers.

During the Christmas season, the REAL SANTA does go to children's parties. He is on the lookout for good girls and boys at malls, schools, skating rinks, hospitals, homes, everywhere. Sometimes he does this Santa work himself. Other times he has his representatives do this on his behalf.

Have you ever thought, "Hey! I just saw Santa!

Wait ... was that the REAL SANTA?"

Well- equipped to have everything needed.

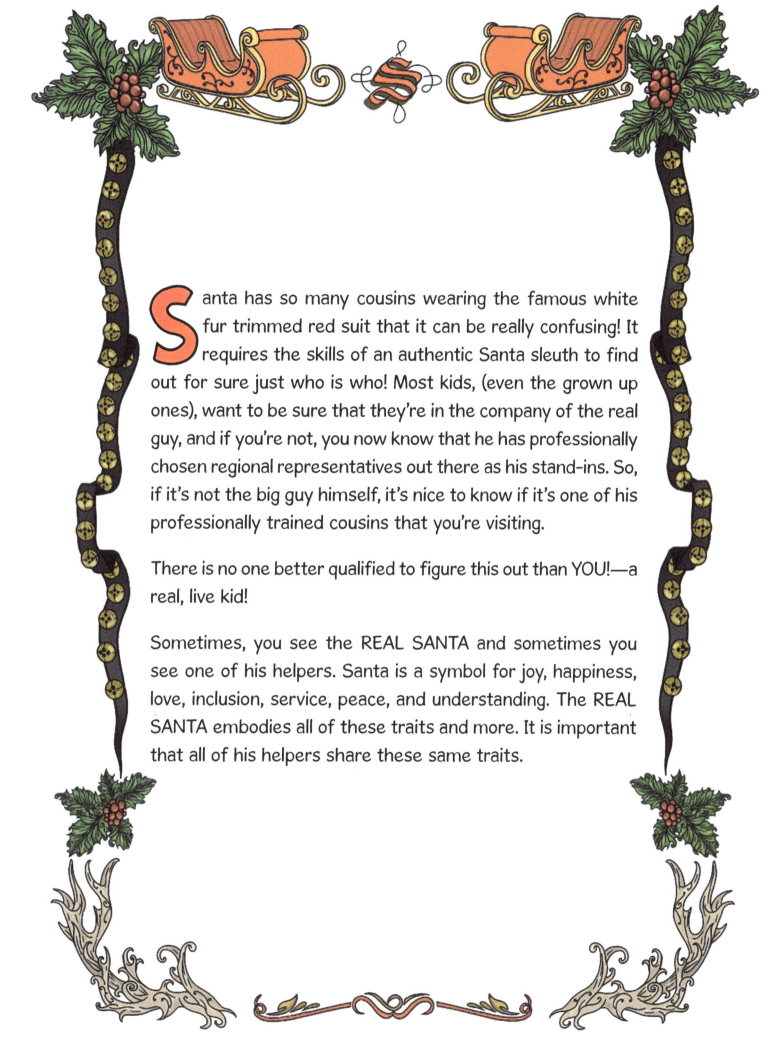

Santa has so many cousins wearing the famous white fur trimmed red suit that it can be really confusing! It requires the skills of an authentic Santa sleuth to find out for sure just who is who! Most kids, (even the grown up ones), want to be sure that they're in the company of the real guy, and if you're not, you now know that he has professionally chosen regional representatives out there as his stand-ins. So, if it's not the big guy himself, it's nice to know if it's one of his professionally trained cousins that you're visiting.

There is no one better qualified to figure this out than YOU!—a real, live kid!

Sometimes, you see the REAL SANTA and sometimes you see one of his helpers. Santa is a symbol for joy, happiness, love, inclusion, service, peace, and understanding. The REAL SANTA embodies all of these traits and more. It is important that all of his helpers share these same traits.

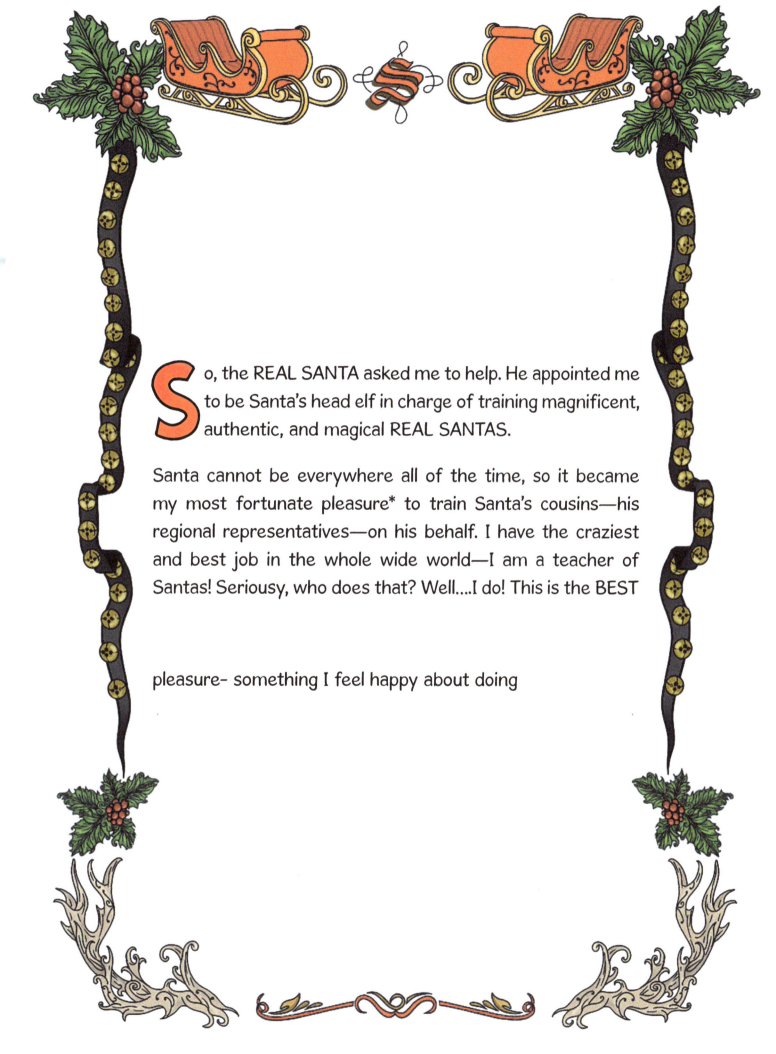

So, the REAL SANTA asked me to help. He appointed me to be Santa's head elf in charge of training magnificent, authentic, and magical REAL SANTAS.

Santa cannot be everywhere all of the time, so it became my most fortunate pleasure* to train Santa's cousins—his regional representatives—on his behalf. I have the craziest and best job in the whole wide world—I am a teacher of Santas! Seriousy, who does that? Well....I do! This is the BEST

pleasure- something I feel happy about doing

I am the Dean of Santa School. Yes, you heard that right. I am not a jolly chubby bearded man. Actually, I am a girl. I am a mom, a sister, a wife, a daughter, and an auntie. I do know Santa and I know what it means to be the REAL SANTA. After all, I am his cousin and Santa himself has taught me all there is to know to really understand what this means and then I get to teach it to others. In short, I am in charge of Santa and that's pretty cool.

I help choose, train, mold, show, and teach good men how to transform* into amazing stand-ins for Santa when he cannot be in attendance himself. These North Pole inspired enthusiasts are people that help spread love and kindness and are very much like the REAL SANTA.

There is a lot that goes into being the REAL SANTA. We have very in-depth studies and rigorous* training at Santa School. In this manual, I am about to disclose* some of their Santa School studies to you so that it will help you in your quest* for finding your REAL SANTA. I know that Santa exists and its up to you, a real live kid, to find him for yourself.

rigorous—exact, precise, thorough, demanding, accurate
disclose—tell a secret
quest—a mission or journey
transform- make a big change in the nature or appearance of something or someone.

Santa School Secrets 101*:

We teach them how to whiten their hair and their beards, so they can look just like Santa. If they do not have their own hair or beards, we introduce them to the best kinds to buy, and the best ways to apply them. You probably did not know this, but sometimes, the REAL SANTA does not have hair or a beard either. Sometimes he needs a hair break and shaves it off and starts fresh again. He taught me to teach the students the best ways to replace hair and beards, temporarily, before they grow in again.

101- a way of telling you that this is a starter course.

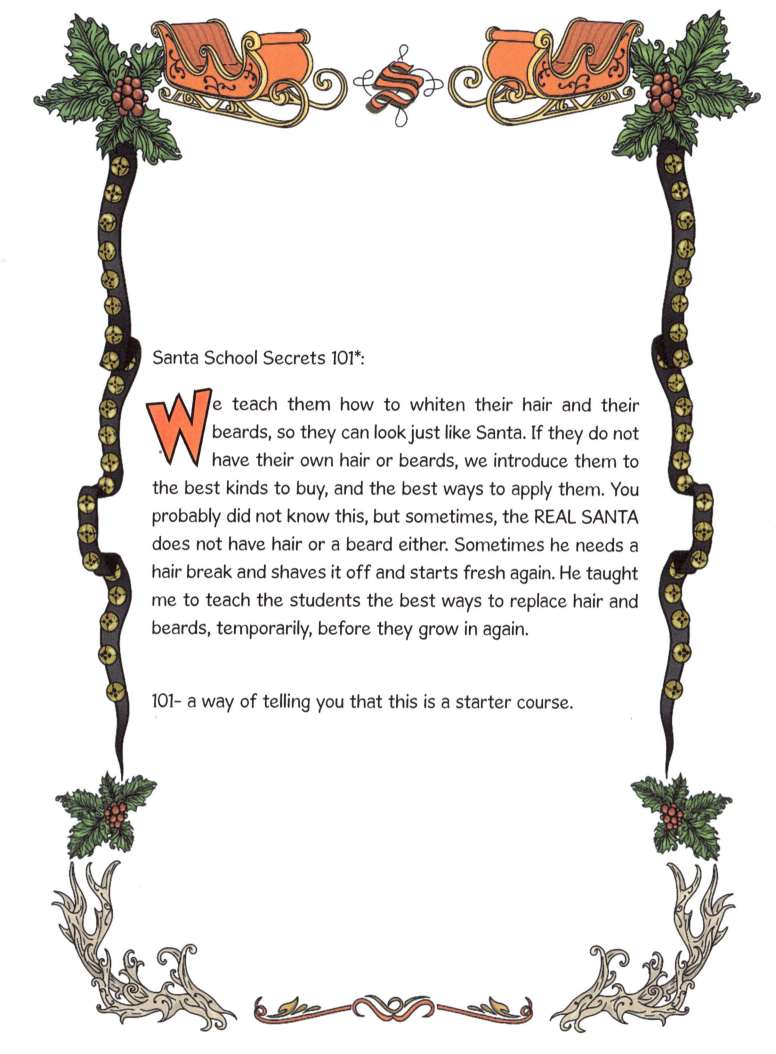

We teach them how to have bellies just like Santa because some of them have small bellies. They have not eaten as many cookies as the REAL SANTA. We help them do this, and we know how because sometimes the REAL SANTA does not have a real belly either. This is a giant secret, too, but the size of his belly kind of depends on Santa's exercise and training program. Sometimes he is better at exercising and eating healthy foods than at other times. Santa does tends to binge on cookies from time to time.

We outfit them in the best and most regal suits and show them how to have shiny boots, magnificent belts, buckles, socks, glasses, bells, and suits, just like the REAL SANTA.

We show them how to be dancers (they're very funny when they try to be like ballerinas), so they can move just like a bowl full of jelly. We practice with them how to read 'Twas the Night Before Christmas' well so that kids have fun hearing the story when they hear it right from Santa's mouth, and we help him to have his little mouth to be drawn up like a bow, just like the story tells. We even show them how to use make up to have their cheeks look rosy and their noses look like cherries. Yes, fun fact, sometimes Santa and his helpers do wear make up!

regal- fit for a king, magnificent.

We even have professional coaches to help them be on their tippiest tip toes when you and other children ask these Santas the hard questions. They need to be prepared! The coaching also helps them prepare for those times when Santa has something unexpected happen like getting gum all over his suit or times when children might have upset tummies and barf right on Santa's suit. Also, how he recovers from a fall. These things happen.

**S**anta has asked me to train these students to be very Santa-like, but he also wants them to be their own special version of Mr Claus. We hope they will be like snowflakes: special, different, and unique.

Santa hopes the same for all the children. You are all special and wonderful just the way you are.


unique- one of its kind.

We do not want robot or cookie cutter Santas, which means that we want their beautiful personalities to shine through their Santa character! So, we work on that too.

Of course, they cannot graduate from Santa School until they have their "Ho Ho Hos" nailed! Santa's Ho Ho Ho is not random. Some people have the misconception* that Santa says this word 'Ho' three distinct* times. This is not true at all. Santa's famous signature "Ho Ho Ho" is his famous laugh. It can be short or long, loud or soft, quizzical* or funny. We practice this until the Santas faces are as red as Rudolph's nose and when we all feel that they are really laughing.

The Santa students also get to meet Santa's reindeer. This is important. How could they stand in for Santa in a pinch if they did not know how to wrangle reindeer? The reindeer have to know these regional representatives and have to be ready to work with any and all of our students. They must be well versed* in all things Santa.

misconception- an idea based on a wrong thought

It is not only about how they look. They must have the kind of warm, kind heart that makes their eyes sparkle and become magical. Their eyes do have to twinkle and their dimples if they have them, do in fact need to be merry! The warmth and kindness of a person is stored in their heart and shines through their eyes. This is very important for Santa and his representatives because they exist to make children of all ages happy.

Sometimes children ask Santa difficult questions. We try to help our Santa students with that too. We have answers for many questions. Unfortunately, some questions cannot be answered and some wishes cannot be granted. So for those times, we teach the Santas how to be great listeners.

Santa's best representatives are kind and considerate. They are also eager* learners. They want to be as much like the REAL SANTA as possible, so they work hard to be better every day—like we all should do.

We teach Santa's representatives how to use their Santa voices, how to engage* their purposeful* Santa walks, and how to enter and exit a room as much like the REAL SANTA as possible.

engage- find and start
Eager- purposeful-showing determination

The Santa students learn the best way for good girls and boys to sit on a Santa's lap for a visit. We want you and the other children to always feel comfortable, safe, and at home with Santa. He should be an adult you can trust.

We believe Santa is a part of everybody's family—not just my family. We believe that he is one of the links to the human family. What we mean by this is that he is the common denominator for good. What is important for all of us is that we are good and kind and try to do a little better everyday. For these reasons, Santa is all of our common family member.

There is something we teach at Santa School you might think is kind of silly. It will make sense when you imagine Santa in your mind.... He can't be stinky. He needs to smell like Santa.

Santa is always clean and tidy. His breath should smell like candy canes or cinnamon and his suit should smell like gingerbread or a Christmas tree of course. These are the happy, cozy smells of Christmas time.

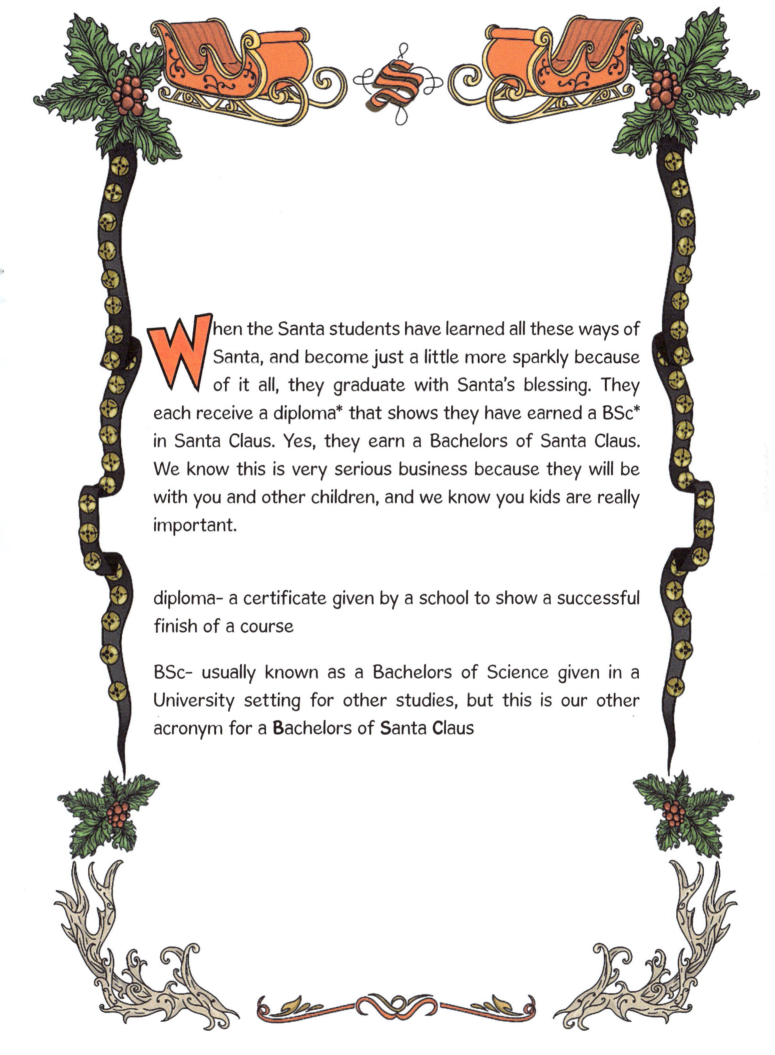

When the Santa students have learned all these ways of Santa, and become just a little more sparkly because of it all, they graduate with Santa's blessing. They each receive a diploma* that shows they have earned a BSc* in Santa Claus. Yes, they earn a Bachelors of Santa Claus. We know this is very serious business because they will be with you and other children, and we know you kids are really important.

diploma- a certificate given by a school to show a successful finish of a course

BSc- usually known as a Bachelors of Science given in a University setting for other studies, but this is our other acronym for a **B**achelors of **S**anta **C**laus

Most importantly, they have to be like REAL SANTA:

**R**emarkable

**E**xceptional

**A**uthentic

**L**istener

**S**ervice

**A**ccepting

**N**oble

**T**rustworthy

**A**geless

So, when you are on your quest to find the REAL SANTA, remember this manual, made just for you. In your travels as a Santa specialist, remember to be nice. We never want to hurt the feelings of one of Santa's cousins in red. Always be respectful. These trained representatives are on Santa's errand* and they will give their recommendation* lists of the good girls and boys to the big guy. Remember, this could also be the REAL SANTA you are meeting.

recommendation- suggestions
Errand- a short journey to deliver or collect something

Here are a few reminders on your quest for the REAL big man in red ...

~Ask him some tough questions.
~See if he has rosy cheeks and a nose a bit like a cherry.

~Look at his hair and beard. Are they soft and snowy white? Remember, it is okay if they are fake. That is another top secret about Santa you learned here.

~Listen. Does he sound like Santa? Does he say the things Santa would say?

~Determine* if his laugh is authentic*. Does it sound like Santa's Ho Ho Ho?

~And of course, never forget ... the SNIFF TEST!

**D**id you ever think or ask Santa, "Are you the REAL SANTA?"

I did. One day, when I was a little girl, sitting on Santa's lap, I asked him that very question.

Santa looked at me over his glasses. He smiled kindly and thoughtfully and then answered back, "Jenny, are you the real you?"

"Yes Santa, I am the real me," I said.

"If you are the real you Jenny, then I must be the real me."

Jennifer Andrews is a Believer. She is a proud mom, wife, daughter, auntie, and sister. She has never had to have 'the talk' about Santa, because in her home, Santa is very real.

Jennifer has been teaching other believers how to become Santa when Santa cannot be there himself. She is the Dean of Santa School in Calgary, Alberta, Canada and has taught hundreds of Santa's Regional Representatives from all over the world.

She knows that there is indeed the real Santa, and its up to each person to discover who or where their real Santa is found!

CPSIA information can be obtained
at www.ICGtesting.com
Printed in the USA
LVHW070302031120
670549LV00003B/33